THAT IS IT YES!

FOR MY HUSBAND

MICHELLE HAS AN IDEA

MICHELLE REMEMBERS THAT GOOD PET, AS HE STILL HAS THE BAD PET WAS AND A SHORT STORY COLLECTION FOR 20 YEAR RELEASED JUBILAEUM A MUSIC GROUP (BASED ON A TRUE STORY, THERE ARE SHORT STORIES ABOUT PEOPLE OF DIFFERENT NATIONALITIES, WHICH CONNECTS ONE THING: THE

MUSIC) AND A MUSICIANS OF THIS BAND HAS COME TO KNOW. AND HER HUSBAND, XAVIER, THE ARTIST, SHORT X, ONE OF THE MUSICIANS OF THE BAND HAS WHEN OCCURS MET OVERSEAS. LAKE HE CALLS HIMSELF AND HE HAS TODAY, 16 NOVEMBER BIRTHDAY.

YOU ARE CONSIDERING HAS TO CONGRATULATE THE MUSICIANS ON A VERY SPECIAL WAY IN WHICH IT. AN IMAGE OF X AND PUBLISHED IT IN A SOCIAL NETWORK THIS IS ALSO GOOD FOR THE FOUNDATION OF AMBER. GOOD PET AND BUNNIES HIS WIFE ARE THRILLED.

AMBER IS LAUGHING

GOOD PET AND BUNNIES ARE SOME TIME AGO MOVED OUT OF THE WG TO SAMMY PROJECT TO HELP WITH HIS SOCIAL. HE HAS ASKED FOR HELP. YOU HAVE A FEW MONTHS WITH HIM ACCUSTOMED, BUT SAMMY'S FOR A FEW MONTHS IN A WAY TRAVEL GONE, ALWAYS ON THE SPOT WHERE THERE IS

NEED. THERE HE MET KIRA BIEN WHO SERVED AS AMBASSADOR JUST IN THE JUNGLE. THE WELL-KNOWN ACTRESS AND HER HUSBAND, NICK SICK, ALSO A WELL KNOWN ACTOR, HAVE PACKED THEIR THINGS ARE AFTER PETCITY AND HAVE ROTATED ALONG WITH THE CUTE PETS A MOVIE. IN ANY CASE, GOOD PET AND BUNNY DRAWN BACK INTO THE WG, BUT YOUR ROOM IS RENTED TO A NEW

ROOMMATE - AMBER, THE ACROBAT AND ARTIST - BUT NO PROBLEM. YOU AND KITTY ARE THE ONLY SINGLES OF MUSICIANS, ARTISTS, AUTHORS AND DESIGNERS COMMUNITY AND THE TWO GIRLS NOW SHARING A ROOM. GOOD PET AND BUNNIES ARE BACK IN THEIR OLD ROOMS, THE CUTE PETS ARE NOW INCLUDING THE GLOBE-TROTTING SAMMY TO 11 AS AMBER HEARD FROM

MICHELLE'S IDEA, SHE WAS VERY HAPPY.

KITTY AND HER FRIENDS

KITTYS PROMINENT GIRLFRIENDS, THE STARS OF THE 10-PART CHILDREN'S BOOK SERIES SO ISSES GO IN SWITZERLAND TO THE INTERNAT. KITTY, HOWEVER, HAS THE DIGITAL MEDIA CONTACT WITH THE GIRLS, ALSO SHE WAS A FEW MONTHS AGO ON A VISIT TO SWITZERLAND.

YOU AND MICHELLE LOOK AT PICTURES BECAUSE YOU GET THE IDEA FOR A NEW BOOK: SO ISSES! IS THE TITLE. KITTY HAS TO LAUGH. AMBER AND KITTY CHATTING WITH THE THREE IN SWITZERLAND WHO FIND THIS IDEA VERY WELL.

KITTY HAS MICHELLE SNAPPED. SHE KNOWS THAT X A VERY SPECIAL GIFT FOR HIS WIFE HAS PLANNED ...

I ESPECIALLY THANK MY HUSBAND